Traffic

by Melissa Gressok
illustrated by Hector Borlasca

Practice Decodable 21

Mc Graw Hill Education

Bothell, WA • Chicago, IL • Columbus, OH • New York, NY

MHEonline.com

Send all inquiries to:
McGraw-Hill Education
8787 Orion Place
Columbus, OH 43240

ISBN: 978-0-02-145712-0
MHID: 0-02-145712-3

Printed in China

8 9 10 11 12 DSS 27 26 25 24 23

Traffic is still bad.

Finn Radcliff has traffic facts.

I can have traffic facts fast.

Look at the traffic!

Can I slip past the traffic?

Finn Radcliff is not fast.
Traffic blocks him!